Wildlife Watching

Whale Watching

by Diane Bair and Pamela Wright

Consultant:
The Whale Museum
Friday Harbor, Washington

CAPSTONE BOOKS

an imprint of Capstone Press
Mankato, Minnesota

Capstone Books are published by Capstone Press
151 Good Counsel Drive, P.O. Box 669, Mankato, Minnesota 56002
http://www.capstone-press.com

Library of Congress Cataloging-in-Publication Data
Bair, Diane.
    Whale watching/by Diane Bair and Pamela Wright.
    p. cm.—(Wildlife watching)
    Includes bibliographical references and index.
    Summary: Describes the physical characteristics and behavior of different
species of whales and safe ways to observe them.
    ISBN 0-7368-0325-4
    1. Whales—Juvenile literature. 2. Whale watching—Juvenile literature. [1 Whales.
2. Whale watching.] I Wright, Pamela, 1953– . II. Title. III. Series: Bair, Diane.
Wildlife watching.
QL737.C4B226 2000
599.5—dc21   99-22689
                                                     CIP

Editorial Credits
Matt Doeden, editor; Steve Christensen, cover designer and illustrator; Heidi Schoof,
    photo researcher

Photo Credits
Barrett & Mackay, 40
Colephoto/John Schakel, 22
David F. Clobes, 14, 16, 33, 35
Index Stock Imagery, 41
John Elk III, cover inset, 19
Marilyn Kazmers/Innerspace Visions, 38
Michael Nolan/TOM STACK & ASSOCIATES, 39
Mike Bacon/TOM STACK & ASSOCIATES, 46
Phillip Colla/Innerspace Visions, 37
Unicorn Stock Photos/Tommy Dodson, 21
Visuals Unlimited/Glen M. Oliver, cover; David B. Fleetham, 4, 45; John D.
    Cunningham, 7; Joe McDonald, 8; Gerald & Buff Corsi, 25, 28; Mark
    Newman, 31; Ken Zucas, 36

**Thank you to Peter Trull, Center for Coastal Studies, for his assistance in
preparing this book.**

Table of Contents

Chapter 1

Getting to Know Whales

Whales are mammals that live in the ocean. Mammals are warm-blooded animals. Their body temperature remains about the same in all surroundings. Whales spend most of their time beneath the surface of the ocean. But they must come to the surface often to breathe air.

Whales are cetaceans (suh-TAY-shuns). This group of sea mammals also includes dolphins and porpoises. Scientists have identified more than 90 different kinds of whales. Each type of whale is called a species. Scientists split whales into two main groups. One group is

Whales are warm-blooded animals that live in the ocean.

the toothed whales. The other group is the baleen whales. Baleen whales have no teeth.

Toothed Whales

The toothed whale group includes beluga whales and orca whales. Scientists classify all dolphins as toothed whales. Toothed whales hunt prey for food. Their prey includes fish, squid, and other marine mammals. These mammals live in the ocean.

Orca whales are among the best known toothed whales. People sometimes call orca whales "killer whales." This is because orca whales often hunt large prey such as dolphins and other whales.

Baleen Whales

Baleen whales have baleen plates instead of teeth. Baleen plates are narrow, bone-like strips that hang from the whales' upper jaws. They are made of a hard substance called keratin. Keratin is the same substance that makes your fingernails hard. Baleen plates have many small hairs that collect food. Baleen whales eat mainly small fish and krill. Krill are tiny shrimp.

Baleen plates are long strips of keratin that some whales use to collect food.

Baleen whales often grow very large. Blue whales are the largest animals on Earth. These baleen whales are larger than the largest dinosaurs were. Blue whales can grow up to 100 feet (30 meters) long. They can weigh as much as 200 tons (181 metric tons). This is as heavy as 21 African elephants.

Whales' Bodies

Whales breathe through blowholes on the tops of their heads. They rise to the ocean's surface whenever they need a breath. They then blow off the water that collects on their blowholes. This creates a spray of water called a spout. Whales then breathe in air and swim back under the ocean surface.

Many whales live in cold water. These whales have thick layers of fat called blubber to keep them warm. Blubber can be as thick as 20 inches (51 centimeters) on some whales.

Most whales have dorsal fins. Dorsal fins grow on whales' backs. The size and shape of dorsal fins differ with each species. Scientists use the size and shape of these fins to help them identify whale species.

Whales have wide, flat areas called flukes on the ends of their tails. Whales use their flukes to push themselves through the water.

The spray of water that comes out of a whale's blowhole is called a spout.

Dangers to Whales

Whales have few natural enemies. Orca whales may attack other whales. Sharks may attack small or young whales.

People are the greatest danger to whales. Some people kill whales for their blubber and their baleen. They use blubber to make special oils. These oils are used to heat buildings and to cook food. People use baleen to make items such as combs and brushes. In the past, people hunted many large whales until they were nearly extinct. These whales were in danger of dying out.

Today, few countries allow people to hunt whales. But some whale populations remain very small. Scientists are not sure whether these whales will survive. Blue whales are among the most endangered species.

Pollution is another danger to whales. Polluted water kills the food that whales eat. It also can make whales sick. Pollution places whale species with small populations in great danger.

Gray Whale Migration

Many whales migrate. This means they move from one place to another during the year. Most whales migrate north to cold waters during summer. They go to these waters mainly to feed. They swim south to warm waters when the weather grows cold. They mate and produce young in these warm waters.

Some whales migrate long distances each year. The gray whale lives in the Chukchi Sea northwest of Alaska during the summer. In the winter, this whale migrates to the Pacific Ocean near Baja California Sur, Mexico. This distance is about 3,500 miles (5,600 kilometers). This is one of the longest migration distances of any mammal.

Chukchi Sea, Alaska

Summer

Winter

Baja California Sur, Mexico

Whale Size Comparison

Beluga Whale
Length: 15 feet (4.6 meters)
Weight: 1.5 tons (1.4 metric tons)

Minke Whale
Length: 25 to 30 feet (7.6 to 9.1 meters)
Weight: 10 tons (9 metric tons)

Orca Whale
Length: 33 feet (10 meters)
Weight: 10 tons (9 metric tons)

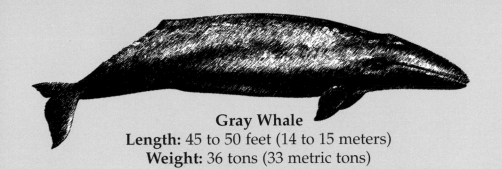

Gray Whale
Length: 45 to 50 feet (14 to 15 meters)
Weight: 36 tons (33 metric tons)

Humpback Whale
Length: 52 feet (16 meters)
Weight: 50 tons (45 metric tons)

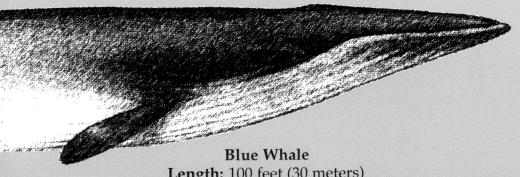

Blue Whale
Length: 100 feet (30 meters)
Weight: 150 tons (136 metric tons)

Chapter 2

Preparing for Your Adventure

The best way to prepare for a whale-watching adventure is to learn about whales. Check out books about whales from your school or local library. Look for nature and wildlife magazine articles about whales. Check TV listings for shows about whales. This will help you know what to look for when you go on your trip.

Study field guides before you go whale watching. Field guides are books that show what animals look like and where they live. A field guide that shows some of the world's whales begins on page 36 of this book.

Find library books about whales before you go whale watching.

Know the proper times to go whale watching. Some whales move to different areas during different times of the year. You can find whale migration schedules in books or on the Internet. You also can write or call companies that take people on whale-watching tours. You can find these companies in phone books, through travel agents, or on the Internet.

Boats

Most people observe whales from boats. Some companies take whale watchers on special tours. These companies provide boats and on-board naturalists. These people study whales. The naturalists know where to find whales. They can help people spot whales. They can teach people about the ways whales behave.

Some people take their own boats to observe whales. Most experts warn people not to do this. This is because it can be dangerous to both people and whales. You must be extremely careful if you choose to observe whales with a personal boat. Whales rarely harm people. But do not get too close to any whales you see.

You can find information about whales on the Internet.

Boat propellers can harm whales that come too close.

You should follow safety rules when observing whales. Never move within 300 feet (91 meters) of a whale. Never place your boat in a whale's path. Never follow directly behind a whale. This may make them feel threatened. Instead, follow the whale from behind and to the side.

Be careful not to separate a whale from other whales in a group. Do not guide your boat between members of a group of whales. You could separate a mother from her young by doing this.

What to Wear

You will probably get wet when you go whale watching. Wear waterproof clothing on the boat. Wear rubber-soled shoes. These shoes grip the wet surface of a boat deck. You may want to bring extra warm clothes in a waterproof bag.

You must wear a life jacket any time you are on a boat. The people who run

You may need binoculars or other viewing devices to see whales clearly.

whale-watching tours usually supply life jackets. You must bring your own life jacket if you go out on your own.

Sunburn is especially dangerous on open water. Wear sunscreen on your face and uncovered skin. This will help you avoid sunburn. Wear sunglasses and a hat or cap with a brim. These items will protect your face and eyes from the sun. Sunglasses with polarizing lenses work best for whale watching. Polarizing lenses reduce the sun's glare off the water.

What to Bring

Proper whale-watching equipment will make your adventure more enjoyable. Binoculars are a very important piece of equipment. This tool makes distant objects appear closer. Binoculars allow you to observe whales from a distance. This helps to keep both you and the whales safe.

You may want to bring a notebook, pencils, and a camera or video recorder. You can use these to make notes, draw pictures, and take photographs and videos. This will help you to record and remember your observations. You also may want to bring a field guide to help you identify whales.

Field guides will help you identify whales.

Chapter 3

Where to Look

Whales live in all the oceans of the world. Many whales migrate along coastlines. Whales may even live in large rivers. Some whales stay far away from coasts in deep ocean waters. Begin your adventure by watching whales that have ranges along coastlines. A range is the geographic region where a plant or animal species naturally lives. Whales that live along coastlines are easier to spot than whales that live in deep waters.

Learn about whales' migration schedules before you make your trip. Summer is the best time to go whale watching in Canada and the northern United States. Whales

Some whales stay far away from coasts in deep waters.

migrate south during winter. You can watch whales along coastlines in southern California and Mexico during winter.

Locations
Popular whale-watching locations in Canada include Vancouver Island, British Columbia, and Churchill, Manitoba. Vancouver Island is in the Pacific Ocean. Churchill is located near Hudson Bay. Whales also are common in the Gulf of St. Lawrence and off the Newfoundland coast.

The coastal waters off Massachusetts and southern California are among the best whale-watching locations in the United States. People also watch whales off the island of Maui, Hawaii, and along Alaska's Glacier Bay.

Spotting Whales
You must be patient when searching for whales. You may have to search for hours before you see one. It can be difficult to guess exactly where whales might be.

Watch for spouts while you search for whales.

When you look for whales, watch the surface of the water for disturbances. Look and listen for whale spouts. Watch the water for dorsal fins and flukes. Keep watching an area if you see any of these disturbances in the water.

Places to See Whales

1 **Lime Kiln Point State Park, Haro Strait, Washington:**
Minke whales and orca whales live off the coast of this park on San
Juan Island, Washington. They stay there from June to September.

2 **Channel Islands National Park, near Ventura, California:**
As many as 20 species of cetaceans live near the Channel Islands.
These five islands are located off the coast of California. Humpback
whales, pilot whales, and gray whales are common there. Whales
live in this area year-round.

3 **Cabrillo National Monument, near San Diego, California:**
People can watch gray whales from this monument. The best time
to visit is from December to February.

4 **White Head Island, Nova Scotia, Canada:**
This island lies in the Atlantic Ocean just north of the
U.S.-Canadian border. Right whales, humpback whales, and
minke whales live in the waters surrounding the island.

5 **Race Point, Cape Cod National Seashore, Massachusetts:**
These waters are located off the Massachusetts coast. Humpback
whales, fin whales, and minke whales live there. The best time to
view these whales is from May to September.

6 **Stellwagen Bank National Marine Sanctuary, Massachusetts:**
This area lies along the Massachusetts coast between Cape Cod and
Cape Ann. Humpback whales, right whales, fin whales, and minke
whales feed there during summer.

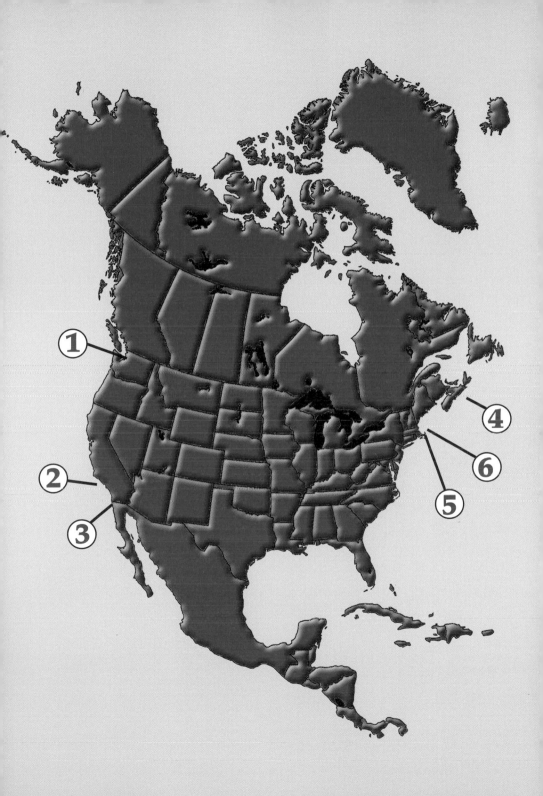

Chapter 4

Making Observations

Observe whales quietly and calmly. Do not disturb the whales you watch. That way, you can observe their natural behavior. Remember to keep your distance while watching whales. Whales may leave an area if they sense danger.

Whale Behavior

Watch for certain whale behaviors. Whales often play on the surface of the ocean. Some may even swim near your boat to observe you. These whales do not seem to fear people.

Whales sometimes jump out of the water headfirst. They then fall back into the water

Some whales may swim near your boat to observe you.

with a large splash. This is called breaching. You can see almost all of a whale's body when it breaches.

Whales sometimes slap their flukes against the ocean surface. They may do this several times in a row. This is called lobtailing or tailslapping.

You may see whales poke their heads above the ocean's surface. This is called spyhopping or bobbing. Whales slowly rise up and turn in a circle. They then sink back beneath the surface.

Groups of some whale species rest together on the water's surface. They often line up in the same direction and remain still. This is called logging.

Whale Calls

Whales communicate with a variety of calls. These calls include high-pitched squeaks, whistles, and clicks. Scientists do not know what all these sounds are for.

Toothed whales also use sounds to find their way around the ocean. They make noises that

You can see almost all of a whale's body when it breaches.

bounce back off other objects in the water. Most of these noises are too high-pitched for people to hear. Whales can tell how close an object is by the way their noises bounce back. This is called echolocation. Some land animals such as bats also use echolocation.

People can hear whale calls with a special underwater microphone called a hydrophone. Crew members on whale-watching tours sometimes attach hydrophones to speakers on boats. This allows passengers to hear the whale calls.

Photographs and Videos

You may want to take photographs or videos of the whales you see. You will need a camera with a telephoto lens to do this. This lens makes distant objects appear closer.

Glare can make it difficult to take photographs and videos on water. Sunlight reflecting on the water's surface causes glare. This can leave large white spots on photographs and videos. You can avoid glare by

Use a camera with a telephoto lens to take photographs and videos of the whales you see.

taking photographs and videos with the sun at your back. Some cameras come with special filters to reduce glare.

Recording Your Observations

Bring a notebook and pencil on your trip. Use these to take notes about your observations. These notes will help you remember the whales you see. Begin by writing the date, time, and place you see whales. Record the number of whales you see. Make notes about each different whale. Record its behavior. Try to figure out which species it is. Describe its body shape and skin color. Describe the whale's fluke if you see it.

You also can record different animals you see living near whales. You may see seabirds flying near whales. You may see groups of fish that whales feed on. Some species of whales may be covered in barnacles. These small shellfish live on whales and ships. Humpback whales and gray whales often have barnacles.

You can take notes and draw pictures of the whales you saw on your trip.

You may want to draw pictures of the whales you saw. You can show them to friends and family members when you tell them about your trip. You can use your pictures, photographs, and videos to help others learn about whales.

Beluga Whale

Description: The beluga whale also is called the white whale. This is because beluga whales have white skin. Beluga whales have small, rounded heads. Beluga whales grow to be about 15 feet (4.6 meters) long. They weigh about 1.5 tons (1.4 metric tons). Males are slightly larger than females. Beluga whales do not have dorsal fins. This makes it easier for them to swim under sheets of ice. Their flukes are wide and V-shaped.

Range: Beluga whales live only in northern waters. Many live off the coasts of northern Canada and Alaska.

Habitat: Beluga whales usually stay in shallow waters. They sometimes travel up rivers to hunt.

Food: Beluga whales are toothed whales. They hunt fish, squid, and other small marine animals.

Numbers: Between 40,000 and 80,000 beluga whales are alive today. They are not an endangered species.

Blue Whale

Description: Blue whales are the
largest animals on Earth. They can
grow to 100 feet (30 meters) long
and weigh as much as 150 tons (136
metric tons). Blue whales have
blue-gray skin with light spots.
They may have brown, yellow, or
gray spots on their undersides. Blue
whales have short, narrow dorsal
fins located near their wide flukes.

Range: Blue whales live in all the
oceans of the world.

Habitat: Blue whales usually stay in
cool, open water. They stay near the
water's surface most of the time.

Food: Blue whales are baleen
whales. They eat mostly small fish
and krill.

Numbers: About 10,000 to 14,000
blue whales are alive today. They
are an endangered species.

Gray Whale

Description: Gray whales have gray skin with white spots. These whales usually are covered with barnacles and lice. Most gray whales are 45 to 50 feet (14 to 15 meters) long. They weigh about 36 tons (33 metric tons). Gray whales do not have dorsal fins. Their flukes are long and narrow.

Range: Most gray whales migrate from the Chukchi Sea northwest of Alaska to waters off the coast of Baja California Sur, Mexico. A few hundred live in the Pacific Ocean off the coast of Asia.

Habitat: Gray whales usually stay in shallow coastal waters.

Food: Gray whales are baleen whales. They feed mainly on animals that live along the bottom of the ocean.

Numbers: About 27,000 gray whales are alive today. They are not an endangered species.

Humpback Whale

Description: Humpback whales are among the most commonly seen whale species. They grow to be about 52 feet (16 meters) long. They can weigh up to 50 tons (45 metric tons). Humpback whales can be white, gray, or black. They have small dorsal fins. Humpback whales have large, V-shaped flukes. Their flukes may have white markings.

Range: Humpback whales live in most of the world's oceans.

Habitat: Humpback whales usually stay near the surface in shallow waters.

Food: Humpback whales are baleen whales. They eat mainly fish and krill. They sometimes work together in groups to feed.

Numbers: Between 10,000 and 20,000 humpback whales are alive today. They are an endangered species.

Minke Whale

Description: Minke whales are the smallest baleen whales. Most are from 25 to 30 feet (7.6 to 9.1 meters) long. They can weigh 10 tons (9 metric tons). Females are slightly larger than males. Minke whales have gray skin. They have dark skin on their top sides and light skin on their bottom sides. Minke whales do not have dorsal fins. Their flukes are narrow.

Range: Minke whales live in all the world's oceans.

Habitat: Minke whales usually stay near the surface of shallow waters.

Food: Minke whales are baleen whales. They eat mainly small fish and krill.

Numbers: Minke whales are the most common baleen whales. More than 1 million are alive today. They are not an endangered species.

Orca Whale

Description: Scientists consider orca whales to be the largest members of the dolphin family. Orca whales can grow up to 33 feet (10 meters) long. They can weigh 10 tons (9 metric tons). Males usually are larger than females. Orca whales have black bodies with white patches. Their dorsal fins are tall and narrow. Their flukes are short and narrow.

Range: Orca whales live in all the world's oceans. They are most common in northern waters.

Habitat: Most orca whales live in cool, coastal waters. Some live in deeper, offshore waters.

Food: Orca whales are toothed whales. They are excellent hunters. Orca whales eat fish, squid, sharks, and even other whales.

Numbers: Scientists do not know how many orca whales are alive today. The species is not endangered. But local populations in the Pacific Northwest are considered threatened.

Words to Know

baleen (buh-LEEN)—a narrow plate of keratin with stiff hairs; baleen whales use these plates to collect food from seawater.

barnacle (BAR-nuh-kuhl)—a small shellfish that lives on whales

cetacean (suh-TAY-shun)—a group of sea mammals that includes whales, dolphins, and porpoises

echolocation (ek-oh-loh-KAY-shuhn)—the process of using sound and echoes to locate objects and food

endangered species (en-DAYN-jurd SPEE-sheez)—a type of plant or animal in danger of becoming extinct

extinct (ehk-STINGKT)—no longer living anywhere in the world

fluke (FLOOK)—the wide, flat area at the end of a whale's tail

krill (KRIL)—tiny shrimp

migrate (MYE-grate)—to move from one area to another as the seasons change

To Learn More

Cooper, Jason. *Watching Whales.* Read All about Whales. Vero Beach, Fla.: Rourke, 1996.

Parker, Steve. *Whales and Dolphins.* Look into Nature. San Francisco: Sierra Club Books for Children, 1994.

Steele, Philip. *The Blue Whale.* Fold Out—Find Out. New York: Kingfisher Books, 1994.

Useful Addresses

American Cetacean Society
P.O. Box 1391
San Pedro, CA 90733-1391

Cetacean Research Unit
P.O. Box 159
Gloucester, MA 01931-0159

Cetacean Society International
P.O. Box 953
Georgetown, CT 06829

International Wildlife Coalition
P.O. Box 461
Port Credit Postal Station
Mississauga, ON L5G 4M1
Canada

Internet Sites

Cetacean Research Unit
http://www.cetacean.org

The Whale Museum
http://www.whale-museum.org

Whale Songs
http://whales.ot.com

Whale Watching
http://whales.magna.com.au/WATCH/index.html

Zoom Whales
http://www.EnchantedLearning.com/subjects/
    whales

Index